T0198984

THERE ONCE WAS A BABY

written by
Patty Ochoa-Malacaman

illustrated by
Debbie Ochoa & Sasha Malacaman

To order additional copies of this book, contact
Toll Free +65 3165 7531 (Singapore)
Toll Free +60 3 3099 4412 (Malaysia)
www.partridgepublishing.com/singapore
orders.singapore@partridgepublishing.com

ISBN
ISBN: 978-1-5437-6980-7 (sc)
ISBN: 978-1-5437-6982-1 (hc)
ISBN: 978-1-5437-6981-4 (e)

Print information available on the last page.

04/20/2022

PARTRIDGE

THIS BOOK BELONGS TO:

_____

There once was a baby
with big bright eyes
Who came to the world
and lit up everyone's lives

The baby was beautiful,
charming and sweet
I loved every part
from the head to the feet

The baby was strong, we knew from the start
The baby was bold- a true lion heart!

The baby grew up
little by little
And the people around,
they started to ponder

4

Will this child grow up
To be a great mighty warrior?

Or a cool creative artist...
Or a sharp-witted teacher?

5

Will this child fly a plane...
Or sail the great oceans?
Or stay on the ground
and make things move in motion?

Will this child dive beneath?
Or climb mountain tops?

Or explore the earth?
Or take care of crops?

But you see, all these questions,
we don't know the answer....
But I'm confident and sure
we don't have to wonder

When the time comes, we will all see

All the hoping and praying we're hoping to be....

Cause this child is blessed
This child is loved true,
This child is mine!

Yes, this child is

YOU!

So be free my dear darling, I'm here beside you

Explore your world and do what you like to do.

Though you fall or you cry or you bruise your leg hard,
Stand up, carry on, stand tall and stand proud

Remember there's always someone behind you,
To love and support you in all that you do

And when you grow up....
you'll still hear my story

About a baby who's loved ever so dearly!

Cause darling, my darling,

You know that it's true...

Always and forever,
My baby is you!

Printed in the United States
by Baker & Taylor Publisher Services